A Tall Wall
The Story of Jericho

We are grateful to the following team of authors for their contributions to *God Loves Me*, a Bible story program for young children. This Bible story, one of a series of fifty-two, was written by Patricia L. Nederveld, managing editor for CRC Publications. Suggestions for using this book were developed by Jesslyn DeBoer, a freelance author from Grand Rapids, Michigan. Yvonne Van Ee, an early childhood educator, served as project consultant and wrote *God Loves Me*, the program guide that accompanies this series of Bible storybooks.

Nederveld has served as a consultant to Title I early childhood programs in Colorado. She has extensive experience as a writer, teacher, and consultant for federally funded preschool, kindergarten, and early childhood programs in Colorado, Texas, Michigan, Florida, Missouri, and Washington, using the *High/Scope* Education Research Foundation curriculum. In addition to writing the *Bible Footprints* church curriculum for four- and five-year-olds, Nederveld edited the revised *Threes* curriculum and the first edition of preschool through second grade materials for the *LiFE* curriculum, all published by CRC Publications.

DeBoer has served as a church preschool leader and as coauthor of the preschool-kindergarten materials for the *LiFE* curriculum published by CRC Publications. She has also written K-6 science and health curriculum for Christian Schools International, Grand Rapids, Michigan, and inspirational gift books for Zondervan Publishing House.

Van Ee is a professor and early childhood program advisor in the Education Department at Calvin College, Grand Rapids, Michigan. She has served as curriculum author and consultant for Christian Schools International and wrote the original *Story Hour* organization manual and curriculum materials for fours and fives.

Photo on page 5: SuperStock; photo on page 20: Digital Stock.

© 1998 by CRC Publications, 2850 Kalamazoo Ave. SE, Grand Rapids, MI 49560. All rights reserved. With the exception of brief excerpts for review purposes, no part of this book may be reproduced in any manner whatsoever without written permission from the publisher. Printed in the United States of America on recycled paper. ✪ 1-800-333-8300

Library of Congress Cataloging-in-Publication Data

Nederveld, Patricia L., 1944-
    A tall wall: the story of Jericho /Patricia L. Nederveld.
      p. cm. — (God loves me; bk. 15)
    Summary: Retells the Bible story of Joshua and the battle of Jericho. Includes follow-up activities.
    ISBN 1-56212-284-3
    1. Joshua (Biblical figure)—Juvenile literature. 2. Jericho—History—Siege, ca. 1400 B.C.—Juvenile literature. 3. Bible stories, English—O.T. Joshua. 4. Bible games and puzzles. [1. Joshua (Biblical figure) 2. Bible stories—O.T.] I. Title. II. Series: Nederveld, Patricia L., 1944- God loves me; bk. 15.
BS580.J7N43 1998
222'.209505—dc21   97-32482
                                                      CIP
                                                        AC

10 9 8 7 6 5 4 3 2 1

A Tall Wall
The Story of Jericho

PATRICIA L. NEDERVELD

ILLUSTRATIONS BY PAUL STOUB

CRC Publications
Grand Rapids, Michigan

This is a story from God's book, the Bible.

It's for *say name(s) of your child(ren).*
It's for me too!

Joshua 6:1-21

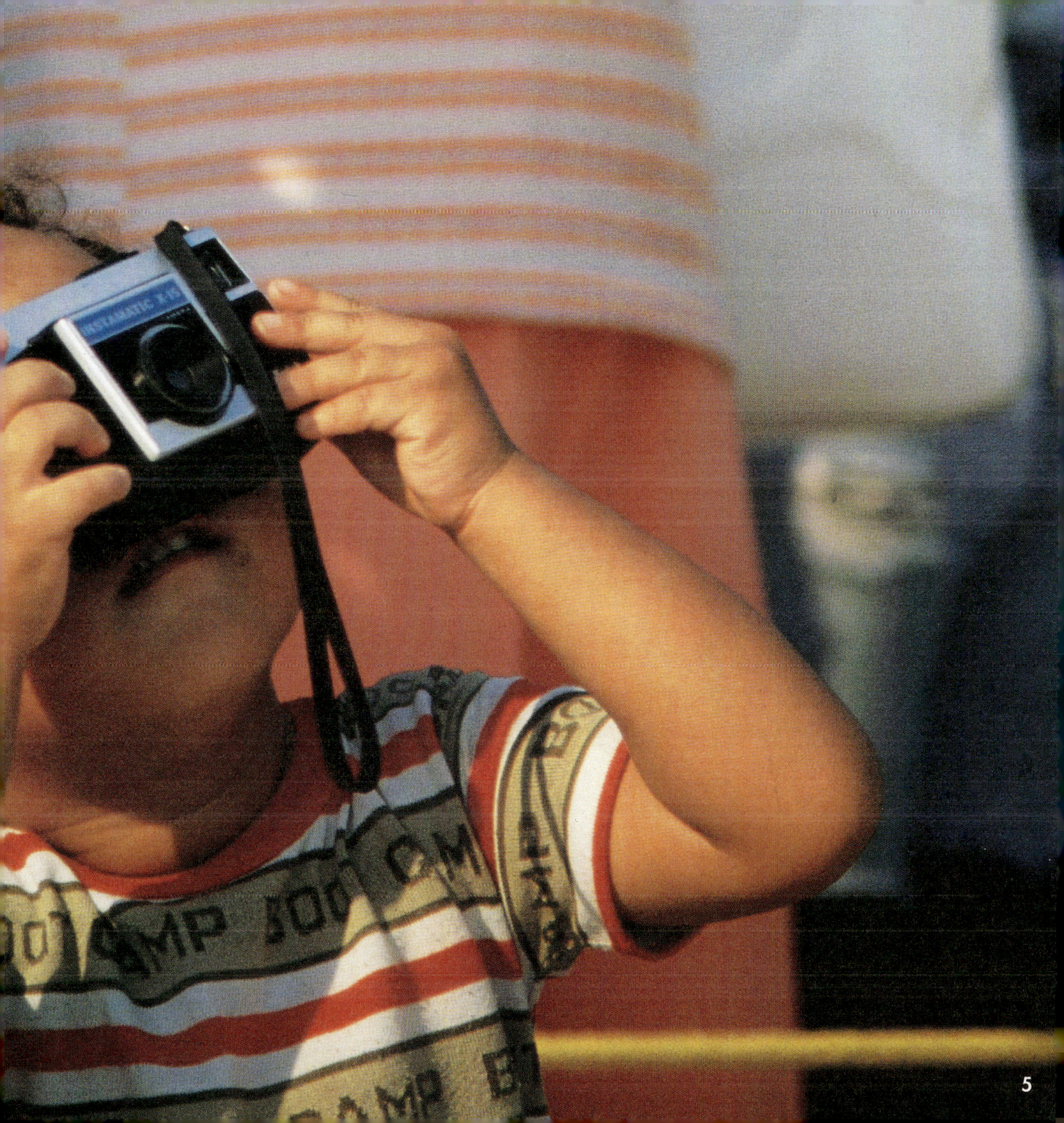
INSTAMATIC X-15

It's an exciting day for God's people. At last—here they are in their new land! Just ahead is the new home God has given them. Everyone is cheering.

God's people see a city with a giant wall stretching all around it. And its gates are locked up tight!

And the closer they get, the bigger those walls look. Way too tall to climb! Way too strong to push over! How will they ever get inside this city called Jericho?

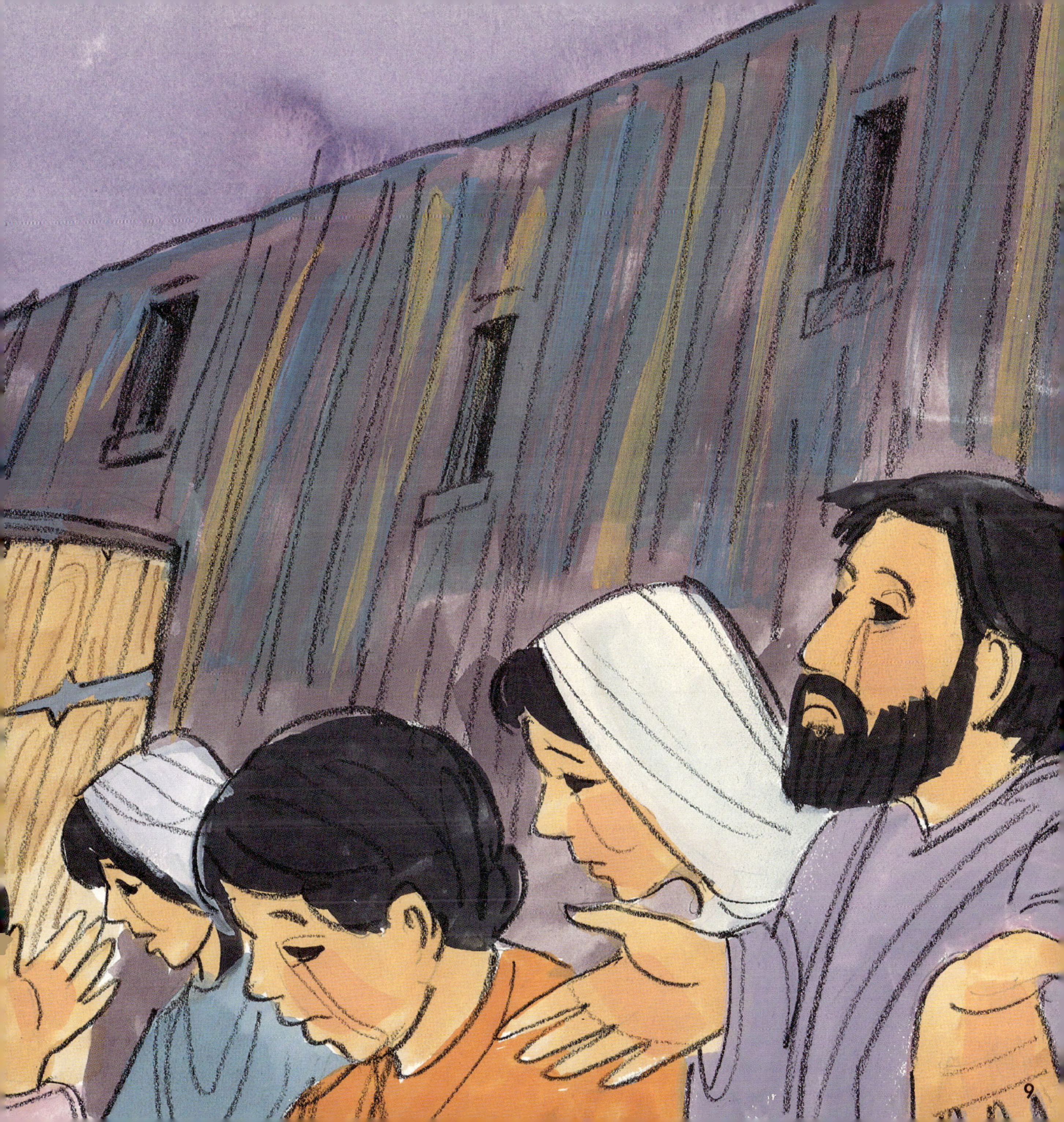

Only God knows the answer. God tells Joshua.

Joshua tells God's people. "Don't worry! God will do it for us! This is the plan . . . "

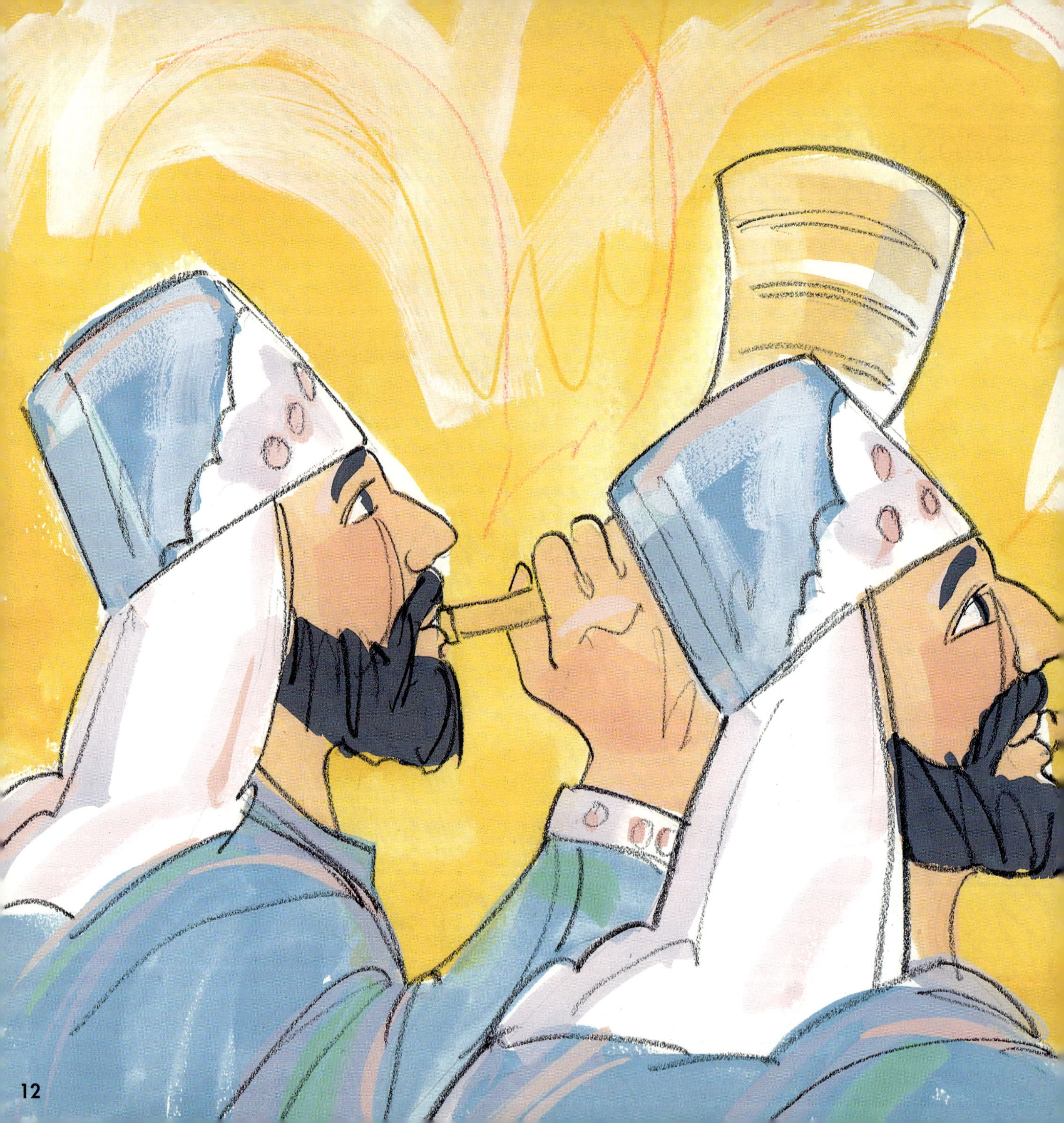

"We'll march all the way around those giant walls tomorrow. The priests will go first, blowing their trumpets."

"We'll follow the priests. But remember, don't say a word until God tells us."

For six days the trumpets sound. For six days God's people march around the tall wall. For six days everyone wonders what God will do . . .

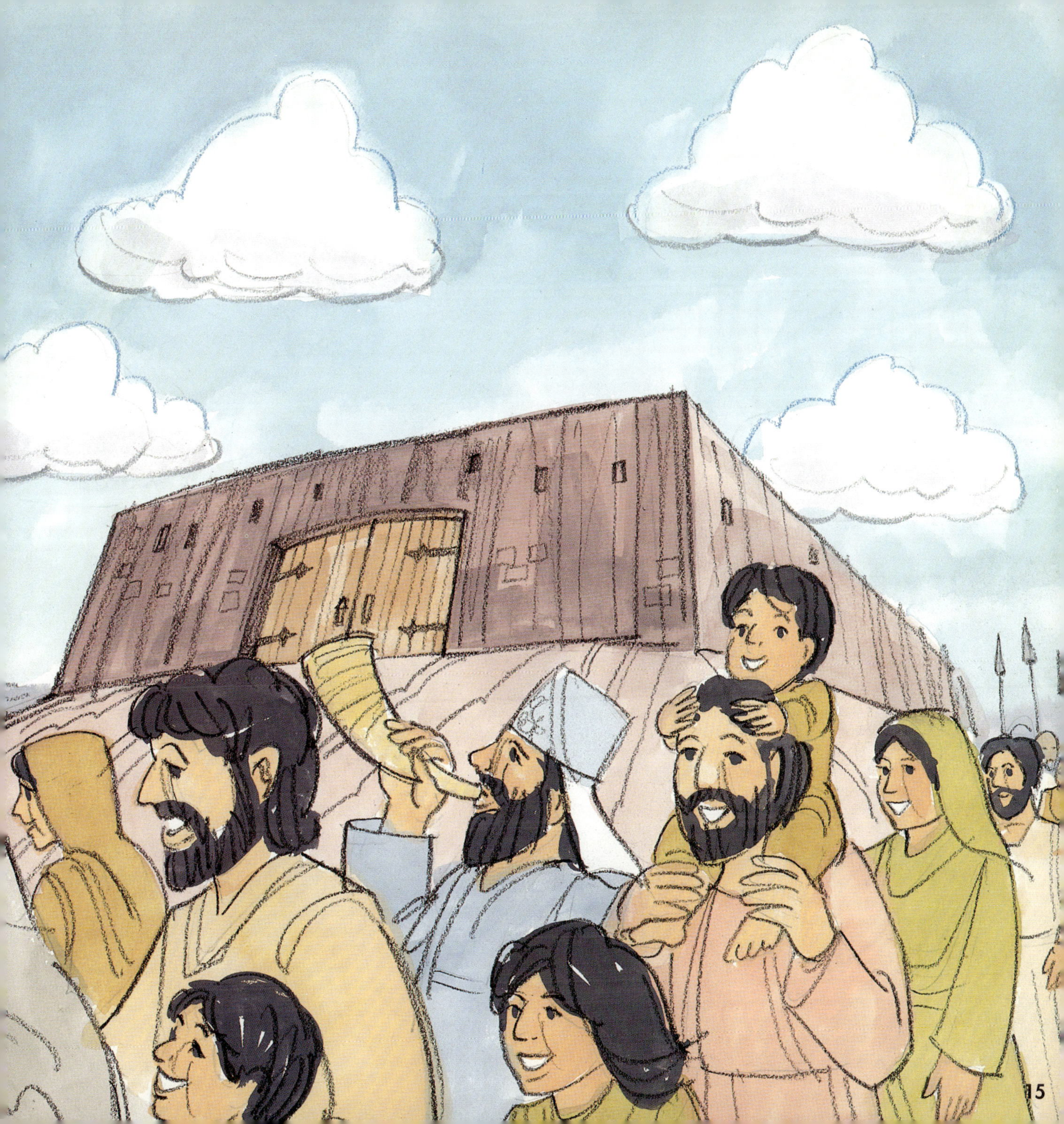

16

Day seven—
the day for
shouting—
comes at last.

God tells Joshua.

Joshua tells God's people. "Shout! Our great God will give us this city *today!*"

Can you see it happening? Our great God is smashing those tall walls. Down they tumble! God's people stand and watch—and cheer! What an exciting day for God's people!

19

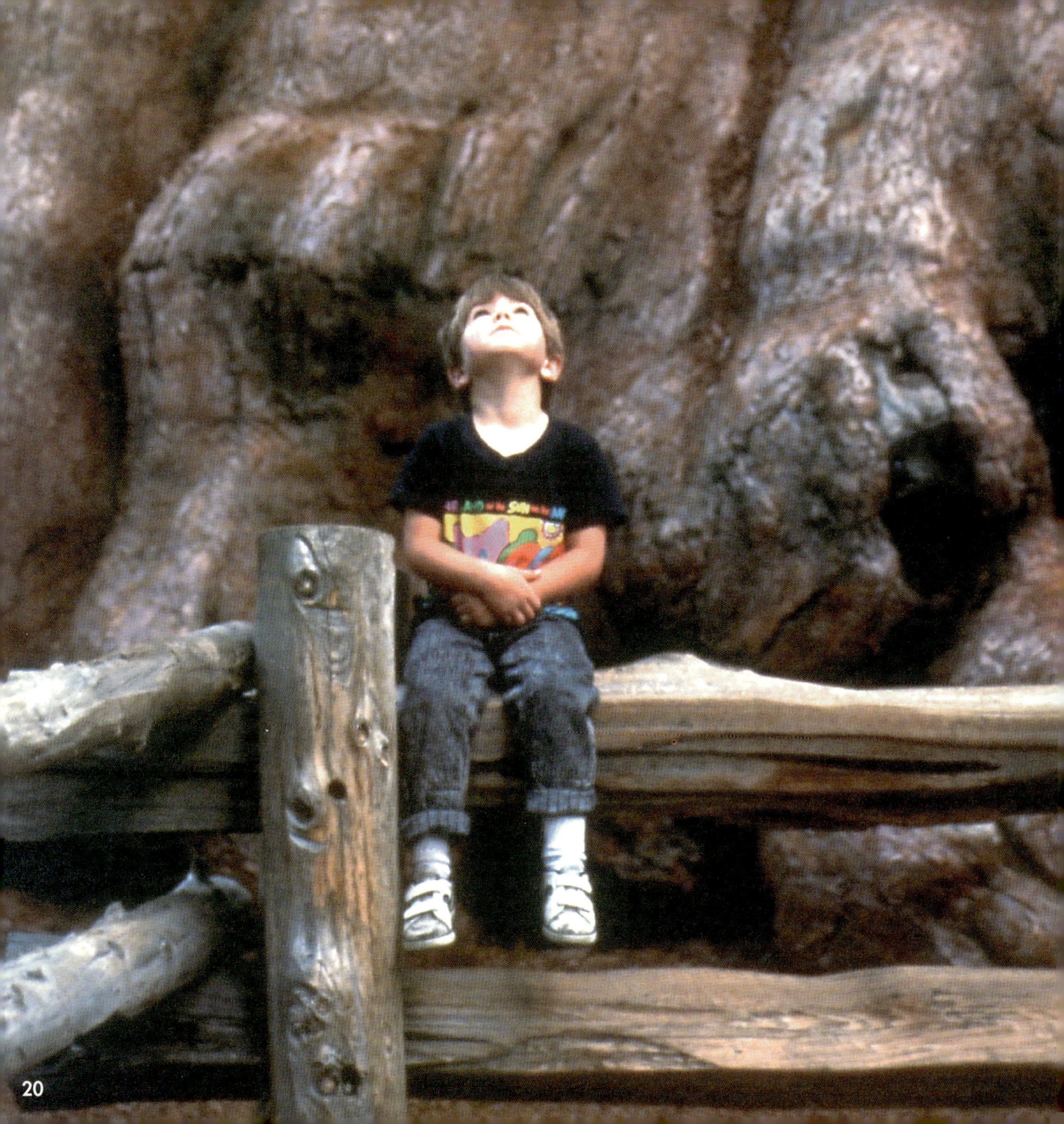

I wonder if you know that our great God is very powerful . . .

Dear God, you do such amazing things for your people. We praise you for your greatness and your power. Amen.

Suggestions for Follow-up

Opening

As you welcome your little ones, give each one a gentle hug or a soft pat on the back. Comment on how healthy and strong each child looks, and tell them how thankful you are for each one. Encourage children to play and learn about our strong God.

Gather the children around you in a large circle. Invite them to do a simple version of Simon Says as you hop with both feet, touch toes, stretch hands up high, and sit down. Praise your little ones for how strong they are. Talk about how boys and girls grow bigger and stronger and about strong mommies and daddies who care for them. Tell them that you know someone who is the strongest of all—our great God who is very powerful and very good.

Learning Through Play

Learning through play is the best way! The following activity suggestions are meant to help you provide props and experiences that will invite the children to play their way into the Scripture story and its simple truth. Try to provide plenty of time for the children to choose their own activities and to play individually. Use group activities sparingly—little ones learn most comfortably with a minimum of structure.

1. Stock your art center with brightly colored construction paper, crayons or washable markers, glue, and stickers. Add scraps of ribbon and lace, and bits of old greeting cards for older children. Invite each child to decorate a sheet of paper with stickers and trims. Write each child's name on the paper. Make trumpets for the children by rolling the paper into funnel shapes; secure with scotch tape.

2. Encourage your little ones to build walls with blocks or cardboard boxes. As you help them stack the pieces, ask the children to describe their structures. Are they tall? Short? Big? Strong? Children often enjoy knocking down their walls and towers as much as building them.

3. Use the trumpets and walls the children have made as props to help them reenact the Israelites' adventure at Jericho. Play on your paper trumpets or rhythm instruments as you march around the walls or the room. Recall how the Israelites marched too. They made a lot of noise, but remind your little ones that it was God's power that knocked the walls down.

4. Sing "Joshua Fought the Battle of Jericho" (Songs Section, *God Loves Me* program guide) either during your circle time or while marching and reenacting the story. Sing this chorus once or twice to the children, and then prompt them to join you every time you sing "Jericho."

5. Read or recite the following action rhyme to the children. Invite them to imitate you as you perform the motions.

   The city walls were oh so tall, (stretch up on tiptoes with arms raised)
   but Joshua's people were so small. (crouch down and look upward)
   The people marched around and around. (march in place)
   Their trumpets made a mighty sound. (hold hands in front of mouth as if blowing horn)
   God told them when to yell, yell, yell. (raise arm or closed fist as in a cheer)
   Then the city walls, they fell, fell, fell. (collapse on the ground)

Closing

Recall how strong and powerful the children were when they knocked down their blocks and boxes. Wonder with them how very strong and powerful God must be to knock down those huge brick walls at Jericho. Remind the children that God is powerful and good. God's power and love protect us. Use the prayer on page 21 to conclude your group time.

At Home

Think of fun ways for your little one to develop large motor skills. Help your child climb over and crawl under a sturdy bench or low fence, crawl through a large box or barrel with both ends removed to form a tunnel, roll in a pile of leaves or down a gentle hill, or carry a small sack of groceries. Praise God together for your child's strong body and talk about how strong and powerful God is—so strong God can knock down walls! Reenact the story of Jericho using empty pop bottles. Stand the bottles side by side in a row to make a wall. Use a soft nerf or rubber ball to roll and knock down the wall. Encourage your child to retell the story with you as you play.

Old Testament Stories

Blue and Green and Purple Too! *The Story of God's Colorful World*
It's a Noisy Place! *The Story of the First Creatures*
Adam and Eve *The Story of the First Man and Woman*
Take Good Care of My World! *The Story of Adam and Eve in the Garden*
A Very Sad Day *The Story of Adam and Eve's Disobedience*
A Rainy, Rainy Day *The Story of Noah*
Count the Stars! *The Story of God's Promise to Abraham and Sarah*
A Girl Named Rebekah *The Story of God's Answer to Abraham*
Two Coats for Joseph *The Story of Young Joseph*
Plenty to Eat *The Story of Joseph and His Brothers*
Safe in a Basket *The Story of Baby Moses*
I'll Do It! *The Story of Moses and the Burning Bush*
Safe at Last! *The Story of Moses and the Red Sea*
What Is It? *The Story of Manna in the Desert*
A Tall Wall *The Story of Jericho*
A Baby for Hannah *The Story of an Answered Prayer*
Samuel! Samuel! *The Story of God's Call to Samuel*
Lions and Bears! *The Story of David the Shepherd Boy*
David and the Giant *The Story of David and Goliath*
A Little Jar of Oil *The Story of Elisha and the Widow*
One, Two, Three, Four, Five, Six, Seven! *The Story of Elisha and Naaman*
A Big Fish Story *The Story of Jonah*
Lions, Lions! *The Story of Daniel*

New Testament Stories

Jesus Is Born! *The Story of Christmas*
Good News! *The Story of the Shepherds*
An Amazing Star! *The Story of the Wise Men*
Waiting, Waiting, Waiting! *The Story of Simeon and Anna*
Who Is This Child? *The Story of Jesus in the Temple*
Follow Me! *The Story of Jesus and His Twelve Helpers*
The Greatest Gift *The Story of Jesus and the Woman at the Well*
A Father's Wish *The Story of Jesus and a Little Boy*
Just Believe! *The Story of Jesus and a Little Girl*
Get Up and Walk! *The Story of Jesus and a Man Who Couldn't Walk*
A Little Lunch *The Story of Jesus and a Hungry Crowd*
A Scary Storm *The Story of Jesus and a Stormy Sea*
Thank You, Jesus! *The Story of Jesus and One Thankful Man*
A Wonderful Sight! *The Story of Jesus and a Man Who Couldn't See*
A Better Thing to Do *The Story of Jesus and Mary and Martha*
A Lost Lamb *The Story of the Good Shepherd*
Come to Me! *The Story of Jesus and the Children*
Have a Great Day! *The Story of Jesus and Zacchaeus*
I Love You, Jesus! *The Story of Mary's Gift to Jesus*
Hosanna! *The Story of Palm Sunday*
The Best Day Ever! *The Story of Easter*
Goodbye—for Now *The Story of Jesus' Return to Heaven*
A Prayer for Peter *The Story of Peter in Prison*
Sad Day, Happy Day! *The Story of Peter ad Dorcas*
A New Friend *The Story of Paul's Conversion*
Over the Wall *The Story of Paul's Escape in a Basket*
A Song in the Night *The Story of Paul and Silas in Prison*
A Ride in the Night *The Story of Paul's Escape on Horseback*
The Shipwreck *The Story of Paul's Rescue at Sea*

Holiday Stories

Selected stories from the New Testament to help you celebrate the Christian year

Jesus Is Born! *The Story of Christmas*
Good News! *The Story of the Shepherds*
An Amazing Star! *The Story of the Wise Men*
Hosanna! *The Story of Palm Sunday*
The Best Day Ever! *The Story of Easter*
Goodbye—for Now *The Story of Jesus' Return to Heaven*

These fifty-two books are the heart of *God Loves Me*, a Bible story program designed for young children. Individual books (or the entire set) and the accompanying program guide *God Loves Me* are available from CRC Publications (1-800-333-8300).